food *style*

noodles

acknowledgements

Firstly, I would like to express my deepest thanks to Anne Wilson and Catie Ziller for the opportunity to write three more books and for having the clear publishing vision that I have been privileged to be a part of for the past four years. To Susan Gray, my patient and careful editor, for picking up all the "oopses". To Marylouise Brammer, the talented designer who has given time, love and dedication to making these books truly beautiful. To Ben Dearnley, the photographer, and Kristen Anderson, the food stylist, for blessing me with their professionalism, friendship but most of all talent for a very special six weeks—thank you for your generosity. To Anna Waddington, project manager and walking angel, for organizing me and my manicness. To Jane Lawson, the new torchbearer, for listening, laughing and yumming with me. To David, Bec, Kate, Lulu and Melita for sharing my passion for food and for making work a special place. To Ross Dobson, Valli Little and Angela Tregonning for testing and tasting my recipes with me and sharing their knowledge. To Donna Hay, lady princess, gifted fellow foodie and friend, just for being who she is. To Mum, Matt, Relle, Rheam, Nathan, Trace, Scottie, Paulie and Kim for their positive feedback, love and patience. To Penel, Michael, Shem and Gabe for a bond and sealant in the form of love that keeps me afloat. To Jude, for doing the yards with me with such honesty and caring. To Dundee for the pearls of wisdom. To Mel, Chaska, Rod, Pete, Fish, Olivia, Annie, Daz, Col, Richie, Melanie, Sean, Anne, George, Yvette, Woody, Ulla, Glenn, Boyd, Sal, Birdie and Dave for enjoying eating as much as I enjoy cooking.

The publisher wishes to thank the following for their generosity in supplying props for the book: Country Road Homewear; Made in Japan; Bison Homewares; Domestic Pots—pieces by Lex Dickson, Victor Greenaway; Empire Homeware; Chee Soon & Fitzgerald; Funkis Swedish Forms; Orson & Blake; Cloth; Craft Australia.

Front cover: shrimp and spinach tempura udon, page 65.

style

noodles

jody vassallo

TIME
LIFE
BOOKS

contents

Dried noodles

soba noodles
Cook in boiling water 3–4 minutes

somen noodles
Cook in boiling water 3 minutes

chinese noodles (wheat) Cook in boiling
water 3 minutes, rinse under cold water

rice stick noodles Pour over
boiling water, soak 10 minutes

udon noodles
Cook in boiling water 4–5 minutes

green tea noodles
Cook in boiling water 4–5 minutes

rice vermicelli Pour over boiling
water, soak 5 minutes

chinese vermicelli (cellophane noodles)
Deep-fry, or soak in boiling water 15 minutes

Fresh noodles

hokkien noodles Gently separate, stand in boiling water 1 minute

rice roll noodles Store at room temperature

rice noodles Store at room temperature

ramen noodles Cook in boiling water 5 minutes, rinse under cold water

flat egg noodles Cook 2 minutes in boiling water, rinse under cold water

udon noodles Cook 2 minutes or until tender

rice noodle sheets Store at room temperature

thin egg noodles Cook 2 minutes in boiling water, rinse under cold water

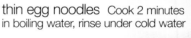

One of the most famous Thai noodle dishes, pad thai is more often than not served for lunch.

pad thai

8 oz narrow, dried rice stick noodles
3 red asian shallots or 1 red spanish onion
3 cloves garlic, chopped
1 small red chile, chopped
4 tablespoons peanut oil
12 shrimp, peeled and deveined, tails left intact
3 1/2 oz firm tofu, diced
2 tablespoons tamarind purée combined with 2 tablespoons water
2 eggs, lightly beaten
2 tablespoons fish sauce
2 tablespoons lime juice
2 tablespoons grated palm sugar or brown sugar
2 tablespoons dried shrimp
1 cup bean sprouts
1 cup fresh cilantro sprigs
1/4 cup roasted peanuts, roughly chopped
lime wedges, to serve

Cover the noodles in boiling water and allow to soak for 15 minutes. Drain. Pound the shallots, garlic and chile in a mortar and pestle to make a fine paste. Heat one tablespoon of oil in a wok, add the shrimp and stir-fry until the shrimp are pink and tender. Remove. Heat the remaining oil in the wok, add the paste and stir-fry over medium heat until fragrant. Add the tofu and stir-fry until golden and slightly crisp. Add the noodles and the tamarind purée and toss until coated with the paste. Push the noodles to one side and pour in the egg. Stir to break up. Stir in the fish sauce, lime juice, palm sugar, dried shrimp, cooked shrimp and half the bean sprouts. Garnish with the remaining bean sprouts, cilantro, peanuts and lime wedges.

Serves 4

Make sure you keep unprepared rice noodle rolls unrefrigerated or they will split when you unroll them.

rice noodle rolls filled with shrimp

Open out the rice noodle sheets and cut 8 6-inch pieces.
Heat the sesame and peanut oils in a wok, add the ginger and scallions and cook over medium heat for 2 minutes.
Add the water chestnuts and shrimp and cook, stirring for 5 minutes or until the shrimp turn pink. Stir in the fish sauce, sugar and chives.
Remove from the pan to cool slightly.
Spoon the mixture down the center of each rice noodle sheet and roll over to enclose the filling.
Heat the vegetable oil in a clean, nonstick frying pan. Cook the noodle rolls in batches over medium heat until golden on both sides.
Serve drizzled with the combined soy sauce, sesame oil and sugar and garnish with extra garlic chives.

1 lb fresh rice noodle sheets,
   at room temperature
1 teaspoon sesame oil
1 tablespoon peanut oil
1 tablespoon grated fresh ginger
3 scallions, thinly sliced
1 cup water chestnuts, chopped
1 lb shrimp, peeled, deveined
   and chopped
1 tablespoon fish sauce
1 tablespoon brown sugar
1 tablespoon snipped garlic chives
2 tablespoons vegetable oil
4 tablespoons light soy sauce
1 teaspoon sesame oil, extra
1/2 teaspoon sugar
extra garlic chives, to garnish

Makes 8

Hokkien noodles come already cooked and are tossed in oil before being vacuum-packed.

crispy seafood noodle balls

6 1/2 oz fresh hokkien noodles
6 1/2 oz shrimp meat
6 1/2 oz red snapper, catfish or any firm-fleshed fish fillets
3 red asian shallots or 1 red spanish onion, chopped
1 teaspoon ground cilantro
1 teaspoon ground cumin
1 teaspoon fish sauce
1 teaspoon sweet chili sauce
2 tablespoons chopped fresh cilantro leaves
oil, for deep-frying
sweet chili dipping sauce
lime juice, to serve

Separate the noodles, pour boiling water over them and allow to rest for 2 minutes to soften. Rinse under cold water, drain and pat dry, then cut into short pieces.
Place the shrimp meat, fish, shallots, ground coriander and cumin in a food processor and process until smooth. Transfer to a bowl and stir in the fish sauce, chili sauce, fresh cilantro and noodles. Shape the mixture into 12 walnut-sized balls, allowing the noodles to hang loosely. Heat the oil until a cube of bread browns in 10 seconds when added to the wok, or until a little of the mixture floats and sizzles when added to the oil. sDeep-fry the balls in batches for 3 minutes, or until golden and cooked through. Serve with sweet chili sauce and a squeeze of lime juice.

This traditional Japanese dish is often referred to as soba but does not in fact use soba (buckwheat noodles).

yakisoba

To make the sauce, place the garlic, ginger, soy sauce, rice vinegar, sugar, lemon juice and water in a saucepan and stir over low heat until the sugar dissolves. Bring to a boil and cook until the sauce thickens. Remove from the heat and allow to rest while you prepare the yakisoba or udon noodles by gently separating the strands.
Combine the pork and sake and allow to marinate for 10 minutes.
Heat the oil in a wok, add the pork and stir-fry over high heat until tender. Add the vegetables and cook until softened. Season with white pepper. Add the noodles and sauce to the contents of the wok and toss to combine and heat through. Serve the noodles topped with pickled ginger.

Serves 4

1 clove garlic, crushed
1/2 tablespoon grated fresh ginger
1/2 cup japanese soy sauce
2 tablespoons rice vinegar
2 tablespoons sugar
1 tablespoon lemon juice
1/4 cup water
13 oz fresh yakisoba or
    udon noodles
4 oz pork fillet, thinly sliced
1 tablespoon sake (dry rice wine)
1 tablespoon sesame oil
2 cups shredded napa cabbage
3 scallions, sliced
1 carrot, thinly sliced
white pepper
2 tablespoons pickled ginger

The Chinese ramen noodle was brought to Japan after WWII and is now the name of a popular soup.

barbecued pork ramen

5 cups chicken stock
1 clove garlic, halved
2 tablespoons japanese soy sauce
1 lb chinese barbecued pork
(char sui), sliced
12 oz fresh ramen noodles
3 cups young spinach leaves
2 hard-boiled eggs, peeled
and halved

Place the chicken stock, garlic, soy sauce and $3^1/_2$ oz of the barbecued pork in a large saucepan and bring to a boil. Reduce the heat and simmer for 10 minutes. Strain and discard the garlic and pork.

Cook the noodles in a large pot of rapidly boiling water for 5 minutes or until al dente. Rinse and drain.

Divide the noodles between 4 soup bowls. Arrange the extra pork on top of the noodles, along with the spinach and egg. Carefully pour over the boiling stock. Allow the spinach to wilt slightly before serving.

Serves 4

Gado gado is a traditional Indonesian dish of raw vegetables served with a spicy peanut sauce.

gado gado with chicken

To make the peanut sauce, heat the oil in a saucepan, add the garlic and chiles and cook until the garlic is soft. Add the remaining ingredients and cook, stirring occasionally, until the sauce thickens. Cook the noodles in boiling water in a large pot for 5 minutes or until tender. Drain. Place the chicken in a frying pan, cover with water and bring to a boil. Remove from the heat and let rest for 15 minutes or until tender. Cool the chicken slightly, then slice thinly. Steam the beans until tender, drain and rinse under cold water. Cook the carrots in the same way. Layer the noodles, beans, carrots, cucumber, chicken, eggs and sprouts on a platter, drizzle with the peanut sauce and serve garnished with onion flakes.

Serves 4–6

Peanut sauce
1 tablespoon peanut oil
2 cloves garlic, finely chopped
2 small red chiles, finely chopped
3 tablespoons crunchy peanut butter
1 cup coconut milk
2 tablespoons kecap manis (Indonesian soy sauce)
2 tablespoons lime juice

10 oz fresh thin egg noodles
2 chicken breast fillets
3/4 lb yard-long or green beans, cut into 2-inch pieces
2 carrots, peeled and thinly sliced
1 cucumber, sliced
4 hard-boiled eggs, peeled and quartered
1 cup bean sprouts
fried onion flakes, to garnish

Sashimi is the Japanese word for sliced raw fish. Make sure the tuna is of the very best quality.

noodle bowls with sashimi tuna

1³/₄ oz dried somen noodles
light olive oil spray
6¹/₂ oz sashimi tuna
1 oz mustard or radish sprouts
¹/₄ cup whole egg mayonnaise
(e.g. Hellmann's)
wasabi (very hot, green horseradish
paste), to taste
2 tablespoons pickled ginger

Preheat the oven to 425°F. Cook the somen noodles in a large pot of boiling water for 3 minutes or until tender. Drain and pat dry. Shape the noodles into small, flat disks, then place the disks into 2 shallow 12-cup muffin pans, pressing the noodles up the sides to form shallow bowls. Lightly spray with olive oil and bake for 10 minutes, or until crisp and golden. Allow to cool. Chop the tuna into small cubes. Divide the tuna among the noodle bowls and top with a few mustard sprouts. Combine the mayonnaise and wasabi in a small bowl. Spoon a dollop of the mayonnaise on top of the tuna and garnish with some pickled ginger. Serve immediately.

Makes 24

Tofu, or bean curd, comes in many forms, e.g. silken, firm, smoked. Firm tofu is ideal for this recipe.

hokkien noodles with asian greens and glazed tofu

Cut the tofu into 1/2-inch thick steaks, place into a shallow, nonmetallic dish and pour over the combined kecap manis, soy and oyster sauces. Allow the tofu to marinate for 15 minutes, then drain and reserve the marinade. Heat the oils in a wok over medium heat, add the garlic, ginger and onions and stir-fry until the onions are soft. Remove. Add the green vegetables to the wok and stir-fry until just wilted. Remove. Add the separated noodles and the reserved marinade and stir-fry until heated through. Remove from the wok and divide between 4 plates. Fry the tofu in the extra oil until it is browned on both sides. Serve the noodles topped with the tofu, green vegetables and onion mixture.

Serves 4

10 oz firm tofu
1/4 cup kecap manis (Indonesian soy sauce)
1 tablespoon soy sauce
1 tablespoon oyster sauce
1 teaspoon sesame oil
1 tablespoon peanut oil
2 cloves garlic, crushed
1 tablespoon grated fresh ginger
1 onion, cut into wedges
1 bunch chinese flowering cabbage (choy sum), roughly chopped
1 bunch baby bok choy, roughly chopped
14 oz fresh hokkien noodles, separated
2 tablespoons peanut oil, extra

Kecap manis is a sweet, dark soy
sauce flavored with palm sugar,
star anise and a mixture of spices.

rice stick noodles with kecap beef

8 oz narrow, dried rice stick noodles
3 tablespoons peanut oil
10 oz butt steak, sliced
2 cloves garlic, finely chopped
1 lemongrass stalk, white part only,
finely chopped
3 scallions, sliced into
1 1/4-inch pieces
1/2 lb sugar snap peas
1 bunch broccolini, roughly chopped
3 tablespoons kecap manis
2 tablespoons soy sauce
1 tablespoon fish sauce
2 tablespoons snipped garlic chives

Pour boiling water over the noodles
and allow them to rest for 10 minutes or
until tender. Drain.

Heat half the oil in a wok, add the
meat, garlic and lemongrass in batches
and stir-fry over high heat until the meat
is browned. Add the scallions and the
greens and stir-fry until bright green and
tender, but still slightly crisp. Remove
and keep warm.

Add the remaining oil to the wok and
then the noodles. Stir-fry for 1 minute.
Stir in the kecap manis, soy sauce and
fish sauce to coat the noodles.

Return the meat and the vegetables
to the wok, along with any juices,
and heat through. Stir in the chives
and serve immediately.

Serves 4

Chinese vermicelli, also known as glass or cellophane noodles, is made from mung bean starch.

chicken noodle larb in banana leaf cones

Separate the vermicelli and break into shorter pieces. Heat the oil until a cube of bread browns in 15 seconds when added to the pan. Cook the vermicelli in batches until puffed and crisp. Drain on crumpled paper towels. Heat the peanut oil in a wok, add the chicken and cook over medium heat until the meat is tender. Add the fish sauce, lime juice and palm sugar, stirring until the sugar dissolves. Remove from the heat and set aside. When cool, stir in the shallots, scallions, chiles, mint and basil leaves. Drain off any excess liquid. Shape banana or lettuce leaves into cones and secure with toothpicks. Fold the noodles into the salad and place immediately in the cones.

Makes 12

1 3/4 oz dried chinese vermicelli
oil, for deep-frying
1 tablespoon peanut oil
1 lb ground chicken
4 tablespoons fish sauce
1/2 cup lime juice
1 tablespoon grated light palm sugar or brown sugar
6 red asian shallots or 2 red spanish onions, thinly sliced
4 scallions, chopped
2 small red chiles, finely chopped
1/2 cup mint leaves, finely shredded
1/2 cup thai, or sweet, basil leaves, finely shredded
12 banana leaves (not to be eaten) or 12 iceberg lettuce leaves, cut into 6-inch squares

Fish sauce—a thin, pungent, salty
sauce made from fermented fish—
is a Thai and Vietnamese essential.

pork spring rolls with glass noodles

13/4 oz dried chinese vermicelli
1 tablespoon peanut oil
2 cloves garlic, crushed
1 tablespoon chopped fresh
cilantro root
3 red asian or regular shallots, finely
chopped
5 oz ground pork
2 tablespoons fish sauce
2 tablespoons grated palm sugar or
brown sugar
1 cup bean sprouts
2 tablespoons chopped fresh
cilantro leaves
9 oz package egg roll
wrappers
1 egg white, lightly beaten
oil, for deep-frying
sweet chili sauce, to serve

Cover the vermicelli with boiling water
for 15 minutes or until soft. Drain and
pat dry. Cut into 2-inch pieces.
Heat the oil in a wok, add the garlic,
cilantro root and shallots and stir-fry
over medium heat for 2 minutes.
Add the pork and stir-fry for another
5 minutes. Remove the wok from the
heat and transfer the contents to a
bowl. Stir in the fish sauce and palm
sugar and set aside to cool. Fold in the
bean sprouts and cilantro leaves.
Place one heaping tablespoon of the
mixture onto one corner of each spring
roll wrapper, brush the edges lightly
with egg white and roll up to enclose
the filling. Repeat until the filling is used
up. Heat the oil in a clean wok until hot.
Deep-fry the spring rolls in batches until
crisp. Serve with sweet chili sauce.

Makes 12

seafood laksa

Preheat the oven to 350°F. Wrap the shrimp paste in foil and roast for 5 minutes.

Soak the chiles in boiling water for 15 minutes. Roughly chop the chiles and place into a mortar and pestle with the remaining paste ingredients. Pound to form a smooth paste.

Soak the rice vermicelli in boiling water for 5 minutes or until tender. Drain well and set aside.

Spoon the thick coconut cream from the top of the can and fry with the paste in a wok until the oil from the coconut starts to separate from the paste and the mixture is fragrant.

Add the fish stock and the remaining coconut cream. Bring to a boil, reduce the heat and stir in the seafood and tofu, cooking for 5 minutes or until tender. Season with the fish sauce and palm sugar.

Divide the noodles between 4 serving bowls, ladle on some of the soup and serve topped with the bean sprouts, mint and fried shallots.

Serves 4

Paste

2 teaspoons shrimp paste
6 large, dried red chiles
2 lemongrass stalks, white part only, sliced
1 tablespoon chopped fresh galangal or ginger
8 red asian shallots or 3 small red spanish onions, sliced
1/2 teaspoon ground turmeric
4 candlenuts or macadamia nuts, roughly chopped

Soup

5 oz dried rice vermicelli
3 cups coconut cream—do not shake the can
3 cups fish stock
11/2 lb shrimp, peeled and deveined
61/2 oz Japanese kamboko
8 oz scallops
31/2 oz deep-fried tofu, halved
2 tablespoons fish sauce
1 tablespoon grated palm sugar or brown sugar
1 cup bean sprouts
1/2 cup vietnamese or regular mint
1/4 cup fried red asian shallots or red spanish onion

A favorite of travelers to Thailand, mee grob should be eaten hot and fresh while the noodles are still crisp.

mee grob

oil, for deep-frying
10 oz dried chinese vermicelli
2 eggs, lightly beaten
4 cloves garlic, finely chopped
5 oz shrimp meat
4 oz ground pork
6 1/2 oz firm tofu, diced
1/2 cup grated light palm sugar or brown sugar
2 tablespoons fish sauce
4 tablespoons lime juice
2 tablespoons coconut or rice vinegar
1 cup bean sprouts
2 tablespoons chopped fresh cilantro leaves
sliced small red chiles, to garnish

Heat the oil in a wok until hot, or until a few noodles bubble on the surface of the oil when added. Cook the noodles in batches until puffed and crisp. Drain on paper towels.

Remove all but 2 tablespoons of oil from the wok. Add the egg and allow it to set, then turn and cook the other side. Remove and cut into thin slices. Add a little more oil to the wok if necessary, then cook the garlic for 1 minute. Stir-fry the shrimp, pork and tofu until just cooked. Stir in the sugar, fish sauce, lime juice and vinegar and bring to a boil, cooking for 3 minutes or until syrupy. Remove from the heat and stir in the noodles, bean sprouts and cilantro. Serve immediately in bowls, topped with shredded egg omelet and sliced chiles.

Serves 4

Roots, stems, leaves and seeds—
nothing is wasted in Thai cookery
when it comes to cilantro.

thai beef salad with crunchy noodles

Combine the soy sauce, oil, cilantro, palm sugar and white pepper and pour over the steak. Cover and allow to marinate for 30 minutes. Remove the steak and reserve the marinade. Heat the extra oil in a nonstick frying pan and cook the meat over high heat for 3 minutes on each side. Add the water to the pan and cook meat until medium rare. Remove the meat and keep warm.

Add the reserved marinade to the liquid in the pan, together with the fish sauce, the extra water and the extra palm sugar. Bring to a boil, then simmer until the sauce thickens slightly. Arrange the watercress, tomatoes, cucumber and noodles on a large platter. Thinly slice the beef and place on top. Drizzle with the sauce and serve.

Serves 4–6

4 tablespoons soy sauce
2 tablespoons vegetable oil
3 tablespoons chopped cilantro root and stem
1 tablespoon grated palm sugar or brown sugar
2 teaspoons ground white pepper
1 lb butt steak, trimmed of excess fat and sinew
1 tablespoon vegetable oil, extra
1/3 cup water
2 tablespoons fish sauce
2 tablespoons water, extra
1 tablespoon grated palm sugar or brown sugar, extra
6 cups watercress
1/2 lb cherry tomatoes, halved
1 cucumber, sliced
1 3/4 oz fried egg noodles

Rice paper wrappers are fragile.
Don't have your soaking water
too hot or the wrappers will tear.

vietnamese spring rolls

3 1/2 oz dried chinese vermicelli
20 egg roll wrappers, about
6 1/2 inches diameter
40 fresh mint leaves
20 large cooked shrimp, peeled,
deveined and cut in
half horizontally
10 garlic chives, halved

Dipping sauce
3 tablespoons hoisin sauce
2 tablespoons soy sauce
1 tablespoon sweet chili sauce
1 small red chile, finely chopped
1 tablespoon chopped roasted
peanuts

Soak the vermicelli in boiling water for
15 minutes or until tender. Drain, pat dry
and cut into shorter pieces with scissors.
Dip one egg roll wrapper at a time into a
bowl of lukewarm water and allow it to
soak for 30 seconds or until soft.
Place the wrappers onto a dry surface,
spoon one heaping tablespoon of the
noodles along the bottom 1/3 of each
one, top with 2 mint leaves and
2 shrimp halves. Fold in the sides and
roll up firmly, enclosing a garlic chive
halfway through each one.
Place rolls seam side down on a plate
and cover with a damp tea towel to
prevent them from drying out.
To make the dipping sauce, mix the
hoisin, soy and sweet chili sauces in
a bowl with the fresh chile. Top with the
chopped peanuts.

Makes 20

baked whole fish with fragrant noodle filling

Preheat the oven to 350°F. Pat the fish dry and use tweezers to remove any bones. Soak the noodles in boiling water for 10 minutes. Drain, pat dry and cut into short pieces. Heat the oil in a frying pan and cook the shallots, chiles and ginger over medium heat until the shallots are golden. Transfer the contents of the pan to a bowl. Add the noodles, water chestnuts, bamboo shoots, scallions, cilantro, fish sauce and palm sugar and mix to combine. Open the salmon or trout fillet out flat and spread the noodle filling over the center. Fold the fish over to enclose the filling and secure with string every 2 inches along the fish. Place onto a baking sheet lined with foil and bake for 30–40 minutes or until tender. To make the sauce, place the kaffir lime leaves, lime juice and butter in a saucepan and cook over medium heat until the butter turns nutty brown. Cut the salmon into slices and serve topped with the sauce.

Serves 10–12

1 whole salmon, boned and butterflied
3 1/2 oz dried rice stick noodles
1 tablespoon peanut oil
6 red asian shallots or 2 red spanish onions, chopped
2 fresh red chiles, chopped
2 tablespoons grated fresh ginger
1 cup water chestnuts, chopped
3/4 cup bamboo shoots, chopped
6 scallions, sliced
2 tablespoons chopped fresh cilantro root
1/4 cup chopped fresh cilantro leaves
2 tablespoons fish sauce
2 tablespoons grated palm sugar or brown sugar

Kaffir lime butter sauce
4 kaffir lime leaves, finely shredded
2 tablespoons lime juice
1/2 cup butter

The combination of chicken and sweet chili sauce is classically Thai in both origin and flavor.

hokkien noodle salad with grilled chicken

4 chicken breast fillets
2 lb hokkien noodles, separated
6 scallions, sliced
1 large red bell pepper, sliced
1/2 lb snow peas, sliced
1 carrot, sliced
3 tablespoons fresh mint leaves
3 tablespoons fresh cilantro leaves
2/3 cup roasted cashews
1 tablespoon sesame oil
2 tablespoons peanut oil
4 tablespoons lime juice
4 tablespoons kecap manis
1/3 cup sweet chili sauce

Cook the chicken breasts on a lightly oiled grillpan until tender. Remove from the heat and allow to cool slightly before cutting into thick slices.

Separate the noodles, pour boiling water over them and allow to stand for 1 minute. Rinse under cold water and drain well.

Place the noodles in a bowl, add the vegetables, herbs, cashews and chicken and toss to combine.

Place the oils, lime juice, kecap manis and sweet chili sauce in a bowl and whisk to combine. Pour over the salad and toss well before serving.

Serves 10–12

The preparation of peking duck is elaborate. Fortunately, Chinese food stores sell it ready to eat.

noodle pancakes with peking duck

Rinse the noodle strips under cold water to separate. Drain and pat dry, then transfer to a bowl and mix in 1 tablespoon of the vegetable oil, all of the sesame oil and the sesame seeds.

Lightly grease 8 egg rings and place 4 of them in a large nonstick frying pan with a little oil. Press the noodle mixture firmly into the rings and cook the pancakes over medium heat until crisp and golden. Remove the egg rings and turn the pancakes over. Repeat with the remaining noodle mixture. Keep the pancakes warm.

Place the plum and hoisin sauces in a saucepan with the water and bring to a boil. To serve, place 2 pancakes on top of one another on each plate, top with snow pea sprouts and barbecued duck and drizzle with the sauce.

Serves 4 as an entrée

1 lb fresh rice noodle sheets, cut into 2-inch strips and halved
2 tablespoons vegetable oil
1 teaspoon sesame oil
1/4 cup sesame seeds, toasted
1 cup snow pea sprouts, to garnish
1/2 chinese roast duck (peking duck), meat removed from the bones and cut into slices

Sauce
1 tablespoon plum sauce
3 tablespoons hoisin sauce
1 tablespoon water

Somen noodles are kneaded by hand and then pulled into long, thin noodles that are hung up to dry.

tuna batons in noodle curtains

1 lb fresh tuna
6 1/2 oz dried somen noodles
1 sheet nori (dried seaweed)
oil, for deep-frying

Sauce
2 tablespoons japanese soy sauce
2 tablespoons mirin (sweet rice wine)
1 tablespoon finely shredded pickled ginger
wasabi (very hot, green, horseradish paste), to taste

Cut the tuna into long batons 3/4-inch thick x 2-inch long. Cut the noodles into 3 1/2-inch pieces, then press the noodles to fit around the outside of the tuna batons.

Cut 3/4-inch wide strips of nori, long enough to wrap around the tuna batons. Lightly brush the ends with water and press to secure.

Heat the oil in a wok until hot, or until a cube of bread browns in 15 seconds. Cook the batons in batches for about 1 minute if you like them rare, or longer if you prefer the tuna cooked through. Drain on paper towels.

To make the dipping sauce, place the soy sauce, mirin, pickled ginger and wasabi in a bowl and whisk gently to combine. Serve in a bowl alongside the tuna batons.

Makes 16

The "long" of this Chinese dish refers to the noodle and the "short" to the wonton dumpling.

long and short wonton soup

Combine the drained and chopped mushrooms, pork, cilantro, soy sauce and ginger in a bowl. Brush the edge of each wonton wrapper with water and place a heaping teaspoon of the mixture onto the center of each wrapper. Bring the edges together to enclose the filling.

Place the stock, mushrooms, garlic, ginger and soy sauce in a large saucepan and bring to a boil. Reduce the heat and simmer for 15 minutes. Strain the soup and discard the garlic and ginger. Slice the mushrooms and return them to the soup.

Cook the egg noodles in boiling water for 1–2 minutes or until tender. Drain. Add the wontons to the stock and cook for 5 minutes. Add the noodles, oyster mushrooms and scallions and cook until the vegetables are tender.

Serves 4

2 small, dried shiitake mushrooms (stems removed), soaked in boiling water for 10 minutes
5 oz ground pork
1 tablespoon chopped fresh cilantro leaves
1 tablespoon soy sauce
2 teaspoons grated fresh ginger
18 wonton wrappers

Soup
6 cups chicken stock
2 dried shiitake mushrooms
1 clove garlic, halved
2-inch piece fresh ginger, sliced
1 tablespoon soy sauce
6 1/2 oz fresh, thin egg noodles
1 cup fresh oyster mushrooms
2 scallions, sliced

Chinese broccoli is also known
as broccoli rabe or Chinese kale.
The whole plant can be eaten.

sweet ginger and chili vegetables with rice noodles

1 lb fresh rice noodle sheets,
at room temperature
2 tablespoons oil
1 teaspoon sesame oil
3 tablespoons grated fresh ginger
1 onion, thinly sliced
1 red bell pepper, sliced
1 cup fresh shiitake mushrooms,
sliced
1 cup baby corn
1 lb chinese broccoli, sliced
1/2 lb snow peas
3 tablespoons sweet chili sauce
2 tablespoons fish sauce
2 tablespoons dark soy sauce
1 tablespoon lime juice
16 thai or sweet basil leaves

Cut the noodles sheets into 1 1/4-inch
wide strips, then cut each strip into
3. Gently separate the noodles (you
may need to run a little cold water over
them to do this).
Heat the oils in a wok, add the ginger
and onions and stir-fry until the onions
are soft. Add the vegetables and stir-fry
until brightly colored and just tender.
Add the noodles to the vegetables
and stir-fry until the noodles start to
soften. Stir in the combined sauces
and lime juice and cook until heated
through. Remove from the heat and
toss in the basil leaves.

Serves 4

Thais enjoy green papaya in salads. The unripe fruit contains enzymes that aid digestion.

crab and squiggly green papaya salad

Place the garlic and chiles in a mortar and pestle and pound until just combined. Add the tomatoes, dried shrimp and papaya and mix (do not pound) to release the juice from the tomatoes. Transfer to a large bowl and add the crab meat and noodles. Toss to combine.

Mix together the lime juice, fish sauce, palm sugar and basil, stirring until the sugar dissolves. Pour over the salad and serve immediately to prevent the noodles going soggy.

Serves 4

6 cloves garlic
2 small red chiles, sliced
8 cherry tomatoes, halved
1/4 cup dried shrimp
3 cups finely shredded green papaya
10 oz fresh or canned crab meat
3 1/2 oz fried egg noodles
4 tablespoons lime juice
4 tablespoons fish sauce
3 tablespoons grated palm sugar or
    brown sugar
2 tablespoons shredded thai or sweet
    basil

Szechwan peppercorns, the berries
of the prickly ash, take their name
from their Chinese town of origin.

hokkien noodles with five-spice szechwan chicken

1 lb fresh hokkien noodles
2 tablespoons oil
1 1/2 lb chicken breast fillets,
sliced
2 cloves garlic, crushed
1 onion, cut into thin wedges
1 tablespoon szechwan peppercorns,
roasted and crushed
1–2 teaspoons five-spice powder
3/4 lb fresh asparagus spears,
sliced
2 tablespoons soy sauce
2 tablespoons oyster sauce
1 tablespoon honey

Separate the noodles.
Heat the oil in a wok, add the chicken
in batches and stir-fry over high heat
until golden and tender.
Return all the chicken to the wok, add
the garlic, onions, peppercorns and
five-spice powder and stir-fry over
medium heat for 3 minutes or until the
onions are soft and the spices are
fragrant. Add the asparagus spears
and noodles and stir-fry for 3 minutes.
Stir in the sauces and honey and bring
to a boil. Toss well and serve.

Serves 4

Galangal, a relative of ginger, is a popular ingredient in Thai cooking. If unavailable, use fresh ginger instead.

fragrant corn, coconut and chicken noodle soup

Place the rice vermicelli in a bowl, cover with boiling water and allow to rest for 5 minutes or until soft. Drain. Place the coconut cream, coconut milk, chicken stock and creamed corn in a large saucepan and bring to a boil, then reduce the heat to simmer.

Add the chicken, baby corn, galangal or ginger, lemongrass and lime leaves and simmer until the chicken is tender.

Season with fish sauce, lime juice and palm sugar. Stir in half the cilantro leaves and serve topped with the remaining leaves.

Serves 4

3 1/2 oz dried rice vermicelli
1 cup coconut cream
2 cups coconut milk
1 cup chicken stock
1/2 cup creamed corn
1 lb chicken thigh fillets, diced into
  3/4-inch squares
1 cup baby corn, halved lengthwise
2-inch piece fresh galangal or ginger,
  cut into thin slices
2 lemongrass stalks, white part only,
  bruised and cut into 2-inch pieces
6 kaffir lime or young lime leaves,
  finely shredded
2 tablespoons fish sauce
2 tablespoons lime juice
1 tablespoon grated palm sugar or
  brown sugar
1/2 cup fresh cilantro leaves

Peel away the tough outer leaves of lemongrass and use the tender white stem for a fresh Thai flavor.

green tea noodles with scallops

13 oz dried green tea noodles
2 tablespoons vegetable oil
1 lb scallops
1 tablespoon grated fresh ginger
1–2 small red chiles, seeded and thinly sliced
3 scallions, sliced
2 lemongrass stalks, white part only, thinly sliced
2 teaspoons thai red curry paste
1 2/3 cups coconut cream
1 tablespoon fish sauce
1 tablespoon grated light palm sugar or brown sugar
garlic chives with flowers, to garnish

Cook the noodles in a large pot of boiling water for 4–5 minutes or until tender. Drain and keep warm.

Heat half the oil in a wok and cook the scallops in batches over high heat for 1–2 minutes each side, or until the scallops are browned on both sides. Remove and keep warm.

Add to the wok the remaining oil, ginger, chiles, scallions, lemongrass and curry paste and cook over medium heat until fragrant. Add the coconut cream, fish sauce and palm sugar and bring to a boil. Reduce the heat and simmer for 5 minutes to thicken the sauce. Return the scallops to the wok. Place the noodles on 4 serving plates and pour over the sauce and scallops. Garnish with garlic chives.

Serves 4

Dashi granules, made from dried tuna flakes and seaweed, are used in Japanese cooking to make stock.

somen nests with eggplant and shiitake mushrooms

Blanch the sliced eggplant in boiling water for 5 minutes, then drain, transfer to a plate and weigh down for 15 minutes to press out any remaining liquid. Pat dry. Soak the dried shiitake mushrooms in the boiling water for 10 minutes. Drain and reserve the liquid. Heat the oil in a large frying pan and cook the eggplant slices in batches until golden brown on both sides. Remove. Add the enoki mushrooms and cook for 10 seconds. Remove. Stir in the dashi, sugar, miso, mirin, reserved liquid, water, soy sauce and shiitake mushrooms and bring to a boil. Cover and simmer for 10 minutes. Cook the somen noodles in boiling water for 3 minutes or until tender. Drain. Place nests of the noodles onto plates, top with eggplant slices and the mushrooms and drizzle with the sauce.

2 small eggplants, cut into $1/2$-inch thick slices
12 dried shiitake mushrooms
1 cup boiling water
$1/4$ cup vegetable oil
$31/2$ oz fresh enoki mushrooms
1 teaspoon dashi granules
1 tablespoon sugar
1 tablespoon white miso
1 tablespoon mirin (sweet rice wine)
$1/2$ cup water
$1/4$ cup japanese soy sauce
11 oz dried somen noodles

Serves 4

Radicchio, a member of the chicory family, originated in France and Belgium in the late 19th century.

mini crisp san choy bau on radicchio

oil, for deep-frying
3/4 oz dried chinese vermicelli
1 tablespoon peanut oil
1 teaspoon sesame oil
1 tablespoon grated fresh ginger
2 scallions, sliced
8 oz lean ground pork
31/2 oz chinese barbecued pork, chopped
1 cup water chestnuts, roughly chopped
1 tablespoon soy sauce
1 tablespoon kecap manis (Indonesian soy sauce)
2 tablespoons chopped fresh cilantro leaves
3–4 baby radicchio, leaves separated
extra kecap manis (Indonesian soy sauce), for serving

Heat the oil in a large wok to 375°F, or until a cube of bread browns in 10 seconds when added to the oil. Deep-fry pieces of the vermicelli until crisp. Drain on crumpled paper towels and set aside.

Heat the peanut and sesame oils in a large, nonstick frying pan. Add the ginger and scallions, and cook over medium heat until soft. Add the ground pork and cook over high heat until browned and all the liquid has evaporated. Add the barbecued pork and water chestnuts and stir in the sauces, noodles and cilantro.

Rinse the radicchio leaves and pat dry. Spoon the pork mixture into the leaves and drizzle with a little of the extra kecap manis just before serving.

Makes 20

Tempura is the Japanese name for a light, crisp batter which is often used with vegetables or seafood.

shrimp and spinach tempura udon

Cook the noodles in boiling water in a large pot for 5 minutes or until tender. Drain. Place the remaining broth ingredients in a saucepan and bring to a boil. Reduce the heat and simmer for 10 minutes. Cut slits in the belly of each shrimp to stop them from curling during cooking. Wash the spinach leaves and pat dry. Place the beaten egg, water, flour and sesame seeds in a bowl and mix gently with chopsticks to form a lumpy batter. Heat the oil in a wok until hot, dip the shrimp into the batter in batches, then cook for 2–3 minutes until crisp and lightly golden. Repeat with the spinach leaves. Drain on paper towels. Place mounds of the noodles in bowls, ladle over the broth and top with shrimp and spinach.

Serves 4

Udon broth
13 oz dried udon noodles
1 teaspoon instant dashi granules
4 cups water
1/3 cup japanese soy sauce
1 tablespoon sake (dry rice wine)
1 tablespoon sugar

Tempura
16 shrimp, peeled and deveined, tails left intact
12 young spinach leaves
1 egg, lightly beaten
3/4 cup iced water
1 cup tempura flour
1 tablespoon black sesame seeds
oil, for deep-frying

Char sui is the Chinese name for honey-roasted pork flavored with sugar, spices and special sauces.

noodle nests with barbecued pork and chinese broccoli

6 1/2 oz fresh, flat egg noodles
2 tablespoons peanut oil
1 clove garlic, chopped
1 tablespoon fresh grated ginger
1 onion, sliced
1 lb chinese broccoli (broccoli rabe), cut into 2-inch pieces
13 oz chinese barbecued pork (char sui), sliced
1 tablespoon kecap manis
1 tablespoon oyster sauce
1 tablespoon soy sauce
2 tablespoons toasted sesame seeds, to garnish

Cook the noodles in boiling water for 2 minutes. Drain well and keep warm. Heat the oil in a wok, add the garlic, ginger and onions and stir-fry until the onions are soft. Add the chinese broccoli and stir-fry until it is bright green and tender. Remove and divide between 4 plates.

Add the pork to the wok, together with the combined sauces, and stir-fry until heated through. Spoon the pork over the greens, leaving the sauce in the wok. Form the noodles into nests and place on top of the pork. To serve, drizzle with the extra sauce from the wok and sprinkle with sesame seeds.

Serves 4

Salted black beans are simply
black soy beans that have been
fermented and then salted.

stir-fried rice noodles with black bean fish

Heat 2 tablespoons of the oil in a wok,
add the swordfish in batches and
stir-fry over high heat for 3 minutes or
until golden. Remove and set aside.
Add the remaining oil to the wok and
stir-fry the garlic, ginger and scallions for
2 minutes or until fragrant. Add the
noodles and stir-fry until soft.
Add the black beans, bean sauce,
rice wine, vinegar, soy sauce, sugar
and sesame oil and stir-fry until the
sauce boils and thickens slightly.
Return the fish to the wok along with
the garlic chives. Toss to combine
and serve immediately.

Serves 4

3 tablespoons peanut oil
1 lb swordfish, cut into
   bite-sized pieces
2 cloves garlic, crushed
1 tablespoon grated fresh ginger
6 scallions, cut into 1 1/4-inch pieces
2 lb fresh rice noodle sheets, sliced
   into 3/4-inch strips
5 1/2 oz canned black beans,
   rinsed and drained
2 tablespoons bottled black bean
   sauce
2 tablespoons chinese rice wine
   (shao hsing)
1 tablespoon rice wine vinegar
1 tablespoon soy sauce
2 tablespoons sugar
1/2 teaspoon sesame oil
1 tablespoon garlic chives, cut into
   2-inch pieces

The crisp noodles add a quirky twist to this old seventies favorite that is making a well-deserved comeback.

crunchy shrimp cocktails

13/4 oz dried rice vermicelli
oil, for deep-frying
sea or regular salt
11/2 lb cooked, medium-sized shrimp
1 small iceberg lettuce, leaves separated
1 cucumber, sliced
1 avocado, sliced
1/2 cup whole egg mayonnaise
1 tablespoon ketchup
few drops tabasco sauce
1 tablespoon water
1 lime, cut into 6 wedges, to serve

Break the vermicelli into smaller pieces. Heat the oil in a large saucepan until hot, or until a cube of bread browns in 15 seconds when added to the pan. Add the noodles in batches and cook for 10 seconds or until puffed, white and crisp. Drain on crumpled paper towels and sprinkle with sea salt. Peel and devein the shrimp. Arrange the lettuce and noodles into six shallow bowls and top with the cucumber, avocado and shrimp. Place the mayonnaise, ketchup, tabasco sauce and water in a bowl and whisk to combine. Drizzle over the shrimp. Serve with lime wedges, if desired.

Serves 6

A thin, brown noodle made from buckwheat and wheat flour, soba is a specialty of the Japanese.

chilled soba noodles with chicken

Cook the noodles in boiling water, stirring so that the noodles do not stick together. Add 1/2 cup of cold water to the pot after 4 minutes, then return to a boil. Drain, transfer to a bowl and cover with cold water. Drain and chill. Place the dashi, water, star anise, soy sauce, mirin and sugar in a saucepan and stir over low heat until the sugar dissolves. Bring to a boil, then remove from the heat and chill. Place the chicken breasts in a deep frying pan, cover with water, add the star anise again, bring to a boil then remove from the heat. Cover and allow to rest for 20 minutes or until tender. Chill. Serve the chilled noodles in bowls topped with the thinly sliced chicken and scallions. Pour the chilled broth on top and sprinkle with urashima.

Serves 4

10 oz dried soba noodles
2 teaspoons dashi granules
2 cups water
4 star anise seeds
1/4 cup japanese soy sauce
2 tablespoons mirin (sweet rice wine)
1 teaspoon sugar
2–3 chicken breast fillets
4 scallions, sliced diagonally and chilled in iced water
urashima (nori flakes), to garnish

crispy noodle platter with garlic pepper fish

Garlic pepper sauce
6 cloves garlic, chopped
8 fresh cilantro roots, finely chopped
1 tablespoon white peppercorns
2 tablespoons grated dark palm sugar or brown sugar
2 tablespoons fish sauce
1/2 cup water

1 snapper (approximately 3 lb), or 2 small baby snapper
all-purpose flour, to coat
oil, for deep-frying
61/2 oz dried chinese vermicelli
cilantro leaves, to garnish
2 sliced red chiles, to garnish

To make the sauce, pound the garlic, cilantro roots and white peppercorns in a mortar and pestle to form a smooth paste. Fry the paste in a little of the deep-frying oil until fragrant. Stir in the palm sugar, fish sauce and water and bring to a boil. Continue cooking until the sauce thickens slightly. Set aside and keep warm.

Pat the fish dry. Score deep cuts into the thickest part of the fish, on either side. Toss to coat in seasoned flour, shaking off any excess.

Heat the oil in a large wok to 375°F, or until a cube of bread browns in 10 seconds when added to the oil. Deep-fry pieces of the vermicelli in batches until crisp. Drain on crumpled paper towels, then arrange on a large platter. Reheat the oil and deep-fry the fish for 5 minutes on each side or until the fish is tender and cooked through. To serve, place the fish on the noodles and pour over the garlic pepper sauce. Garnish with the cilantro leaves and sliced chiles.

Serves 4

Miso is fermented soybean paste. The lighter the color of the soup, the more delicate the flavor.

miso soup with udon and tofu

Place the dashi, water, miso and soy sauce in a large saucepan and bring to a boil. Reduce the heat and simmer for 10 minutes. Add the noodles and cook for 5 minutes or until soft. Stir in the tofu, shiitake mushrooms and bok choy and cook for 3 minutes or until the bok choy wilts.

Serves 2–4

1 teaspoon dashi granules
5 cups water
3 tablespoons red (genmai) miso
2 tablespoons soy sauce
13 oz fresh udon noodles, separated
13 oz silken firm tofu, cubed
1/4 lb fresh shiitake mushrooms, sliced
1 bunch baby bok choy, leaves separated

Ponzu is a Japanese dipping
sauce made from rice vinegar,
soy, mirin and dashi (fish stock).

green tea sushi rolls

10 oz dried green tea noodles
6 sheets roasted nori (dried seaweed)
1 3/4 oz pickled daikon,
cut into long, thin strips
3 tablespoons drained red pickled
ginger shreds
ponzu sauce, for dipping

Cook the noodles in a large pot
of rapidly boiling water for 4–5 minutes
or until tender. Rinse under cold water
and pat dry.
Working on a flat surface, lay one sheet
of nori onto a sushi mat. Top with 1/6 of
the noodles along the bottom half of
the nori, then arrange the daikon and
the pickled ginger along the center of
the noodles. Roll the nori up firmly to
enclose the filling. Cut the roll in half and
then each half into 3 equal pieces.
Repeat with the remaining ingredients.
Serve with the ponzu sauce.

Makes 36 pieces

Published by Time-Life Books, a division of Time Life Inc.
Time-Life is a trademark of Time Warner Inc. and affiliated companies.

Time-Life Books
Vice President and Publisher: Neil S. Levin
Vice President, Content Development: Jennifer L. Pearce
Senior Sales Director: Richard J. Vreeland
Director, Marketing and Publicity: Inger Forland
Director of New Product Development: Carolyn M. Clark
Director of Custom Publishing: John Lalor
Director of Rights and Licensing: Olga Vezeris
Executive Editor: Linda Bellamy
Director of Design: Tina Taylor

First published in 2000 by Murdoch Books®,
a division of Murdoch Magazines Pty Ltd,
GPO Box 1203, Sydney, NSW Australia 2001

Photographer: Ben Dearnley
Stylist: Kristen Anderson
Concept & Design: Marylouise Brammer
Project Manager: Anna Waddington
Editor: Susan Gray
Recipe Testing: Ross Dobson, Valli Little, Angela Tregonning

Group General Manager: Mark Smith
Publisher: Kay Scarlett
Production Manager: Liz Fitzgerald

Library of Congress Cataloging-in-Publication Data available upon request.
ISBN 0-7370-3030-5

Printed by Toppan Printing Hong Kong Co. Ltd.
PRINTED IN CHINA. This edition printed 2001.